DISCARD

Families Today

IMMIGRANT FAMILIES

Families Today

Adoptive Families

Disability and Families

Foster Families

Homelessness and Families

Immigrant Families

Incarceration and Families

LGBT Families

Military Families

Multigenerational Families

Multiracial Families

Single-Parent Families

Teen Parents

Families Today

IMMIGRANT FAMILIES

H.W. Poole

MASON CREST

Mason Crest
450 Parkway Drive, Suite D
Broomall, PA 19008
www.masoncrest.com

© 2017 by Mason Crest, an imprint of National Highlights, Inc. All rights reserved. No part of this publication may be reproduced or transmitted in any form or by any means, electronic or mechanical, including photocopying, recording, taping, or any information storage and retrieval system, without permission from the publisher.

MTM Publishing, Inc.
435 West 23rd Street, #8C
New York, NY 10011
www.mtmpublishing.com

President: Valerie Tomaselli
Vice President, Book Development: Hilary Poole
Designer: Annemarie Redmond
Copyeditor: Peter Jaskowiak
Editorial Assistant: Andrea St. Aubin

Series ISBN: 978-1-4222-3612-3
Hardback ISBN: 978-1-4222-3617-8
E-Book ISBN: 978-1-4222-8261-8

Library of Congress Cataloging-in-Publication Data
Names: Poole, Hilary W., author.
Title: Immigrant families / by H.W. Poole.
Description: Broomall, PA : Mason Crest [2017] | Series: Families Today | Includes index.
Identifiers: LCCN 2016004543| ISBN 9781422236178 (hardback) | ISBN 9781422236123 (series) | ISBN 9781422282618 (e-book)
Subjects: LCSH: Immigrant families—Juvenile literature. | Emigration and immigration—Social aspects—Juvenile literature. | Families—Juvenile literature.
Classification: LCC JV6225 .P66 2017 | DDC 306.85086/912—dc23
LC record available at http://lccn.loc.gov/2016004543

Printed and bound in the United States of America.

First printing
9 8 7 6 5 4 3 2 1

TABLE OF CONTENTS

Series Introduction 7
Chapter One: The Melting Pot 11
Chapter Two: Immigration Today 21
Chapter Three: The Salad Bowl 31
Chapter Four: Challenges for Immigrant Families 37
Further Reading 44
Series Glossary 45
Index 47
About the Author 48
Photo Credits 48

Key Icons to Look for:

 **Words to Understand:** These words with their easy-to-understand definitions will increase the reader's understanding of the text, while building vocabulary skills.

 **Sidebars:** This boxed material within the main text allows readers to build knowledge, gain insights, explore possibilities, and broaden their perspectives by weaving together additional information to provide realistic and holistic perspectives.

 **Research Projects:** Readers are pointed toward areas of further inquiry connected to each chapter. Suggestions are provided for projects that encourage deeper research and analysis.

 **Text-Dependent Questions:** These questions send the reader back to the text for more careful attention to the evidence presented there.

 **Series Glossary of Key Terms:** This back-of-the-book glossary contains terminology used throughout the series. Words found here increase the reader's ability to read and comprehend higher-level books and articles in this field.

In the 21st century, families are more diverse than ever before.

SERIES INTRODUCTION

Our vision of "the traditional family" is not nearly as time-honored as one might think. The standard of a mom, a dad, and a couple of kids in a nice house with a white-picket fence is a relic of the 1950s—the heart of the baby boom era. The tumult of the Great Depression followed by a global war caused many Americans to long for safety and predictability—whether such stability was real or not. A newborn mass media was more than happy to serve up this image, in the form of TV shows like *Leave It To Beaver* and *The Adventures of Ozzie and Harriet*. Interestingly, even back in the "glory days" of the traditional family, things were never as simple as they seemed. For example, a number of the classic "traditional" family shows—such as *The Andy Griffith Show, My Three Sons,* and a bit later, *The Courtship of Eddie's Father*—were actually focused on single-parent families.

Sure enough, by the 1960s our image of the "perfect family" was already beginning to fray at the seams. The women's movement, the gay rights movement, and—perhaps more than any single factor—the advent of "no fault" divorce meant that the illusion of the Cleaver family would become harder and harder to maintain. By the early 21st century, only about 7 percent of all family households were traditional—defined as a married couple with children where *only* the father works outside the home.

As the number of these traditional families has declined, "nontraditional" arrangements have increased. There are more single parents, more gay and lesbian parents, and more grandparents raising grandchildren than ever before. Multiracial families—created either through interracial relationships or adoption—are also increasing. Meanwhile, the transition to an all-volunteer military force has meant that there are more kids growing up in military families than there were in the past. Each of these topics is treated in a separate volume in this set.

While some commentators bemoan the decline of the traditional family, others argue that, overall, the recognition of new family arrangements has brought more good than bad. After all, if very few people live like the Cleavers anyway, isn't it better to be honest about that fact? Surely, holding up the traditional family as an ideal to which all should aspire only serves to stigmatize kids whose lives differ from that standard. After all, no children can be held responsible for whatever family they find themselves in; all they can do is grow up as best they can. These books take the position that every family—no matter what it looks like—has the potential to be a successful family.

That being said, challenges and difficulties arise in every family, and nontraditional ones are no exception. For example, single parents tend to be less well off financially than married parents are, and this has long-term impacts on their children. Meanwhile, teenagers who become parents tend to let their educations suffer, which damages their income potential and career possibilities, as well as risking the future educational attainment of their babies. There are some 400,000 children in the foster care system at any given time. We know that the uncertainty of foster care creates real challenges when it comes to both education and emotional health.

Furthermore, some types of "nontraditional" families are ones we wish did not have to exist at all. For example, an estimated 1.6 million children experience homelessness at some point in their lives. At least 40 percent of homeless kids are lesbian, gay, bisexual, or transgender teens who were turned out of their homes because of their orientation. Meanwhile, the United States incarcerates more people than any other nation in the world—about 2.7 million kids (1 in 28) have an incarcerated parent. It would be absurd to pretend that such situations are not extremely stressful and, often, detrimental to kids who have to survive them.

The goal of this set, then, is twofold. First, we've tried to describe the history and shape of various nontraditional families in such a way that kids who aren't familiar with them will be able to not only understand, but empathize. We also present demographic information that may be useful for students who are dipping their toes into introductory sociology concepts.

Second, we have tried to speak specifically to the young people who are living in these nontraditional families. The series strives to address these kids as

Meeting challenges and overcoming them together can make families stronger.

sympathetically and supportively as possible. The volumes look at some of the typical problems that kids in these situations face, and where appropriate, they offer advice and tips for how these kids might get along better in whatever situation confronts them.

Obviously, no single book—whether on disability, the military, divorce, or some other topic—can hope to answer every question or address every problem. To that end, a "Further Reading" section at the back of each book attempts to offer some places to look next. We have also listed appropriate crisis hotlines, for anyone with a need more immediate than can be addressed by a library.

Whether your students have a project to complete or a problem to solve, we hope they will be able to find clear, empathic information about nontraditional families in these pages.

—H. W. Poole

10 Immigrant Families

The Statue of Liberty in New York Harbor.

Chapter One

THE MELTING POT

One summer day, a baby was born to a woman named Lenor and her husband, Martín. Lenor and Martín were very far from home. They had made a long journey over many miles in order to reach America. Their baby, Martín Jr., would grow up in a new land, a place quite different from the one his parents had known.

It is an old story. It might be your story, too. But in this case, there is something special about young Martín. The year of his birth was 1566. Martín's father was mayor of a settlement called St. Augustine, in what would eventually become the state of Florida. Martín de Argüelles Jr. was the first baby born to European settlers of what is now the United States.

Words to Understand

assimilate: to blend in to a new culture or country.

cyclical: reoccurring again and again.

exiles: people who have left their home country.

illiterate: not able to read and write.

mobility: the ability to move, either physically or in terms of improving one's social or financial status.

Immigrant Families

The verb *to immigrate* simply means to go live permanently in a country other than the one in which you were born. Immigrants have been coming to America for 450 years. Many have come seeking work, freedom, or safety—or all of these. Others did not come willingly. From 1616 to 1808, many thousands were brought to America as slaves, made to "immigrate" by force. Unless you are of Native American descent, your family is—somewhere in its history—an immigrant family.

THE GOLDEN AGE OF IMMIGRATION

The Statue of Liberty that looks out over New York Harbor was given to the United States by France in the late 1800s. On display inside the statue is a bronze plaque that features a poem called "The New Colossus" (see box on page 15). A poet named Emma Lazarus wrote the poem to honor immigrants who would see the Statue of Liberty as they arrived in New York by ship. Ever since then, the statue that Lazarus called "Mother of **Exiles**" has symbolized America's identity as "the nation of immigrants."

Immigration has been constant since the first American settlements were founded. In 1555, St. Augustine became the first Spanish settlement, and the Jamestown colony, established in 1607, was the first permanent English settlement. German and Polish settlers arrived in Jamestown the following year, and the first African slaves were brought there in 1619.

But the "golden age" of American immigration was the period from 1815 to 1915—about 30 million immigrants arrived in that 100-year span. In the first 50 years, the majority of immigrants came from northern European countries like Germany and Ireland; in the second 50 years, more came from southern European countries like Italy, and also from Latin America. Often, one member of a family would arrive first—frequently, but not always, it was a husband or father. That family member would find a job and a place to live, and then he (or she) would send for the rest of the family.

Chapter One: The Melting Pot

There were a few reasons why this was the golden age of American immigration. First, many other countries went through hard times during that period. For example, a series of crop failures occurred in Germany in the 1840s, and there was a huge famine in Ireland from 1845 to 1851. The year 1848 saw political revolutions all across Europe, including in France, Italy, and Austria. All these events served to push people out of their home countries, causing them to seek new lives elsewhere.

There were also events that pulled people *toward* the United States. A major factor was economic opportunity. It was said that in America, "the streets were paved with gold." This refers to the belief that anyone can get rich in America if he or she works hard enough. Sometimes the gold was literal, however: the dream of "striking it rich" during the California Gold Rush drew thousands upon thousands of immigrants, especially from China.

Beyond money, something else pulled immigrants toward America: freedom, particularly religious freedom. Ever since the Puritans arrived in Plymouth in 1620,

Immigrants aboard the S.S. *Patricia*, bound for America, 1906.

Immigrant Families

Immigrants at Ellis Island in 1904.

people have been traveling to America because it is a place where people are allowed to worship however they want. In the 19th century, millions of Jews fled religious persecution in Russia and other places. The principles of religious freedom and freedom of speech are such important American values that they are written into the U.S. Constitution as worthy of special protection.

Other immigrants came to America for the adventure of beginning a new life. In this era, there was more **mobility** in the United States than anywhere else in the world. People could "move" up the social ladder, they could "move" up economically, and they could literally move across the massively expanding western frontier. To people in the 19th century, America seemed a place where anything was possible. That was the idea, at least. While the dream has rewarded many immigrants with success, the reality for others has not always been quite so pleasant or pretty.

ANTI-IMMIGRATION ARGUMENTS

There is a famous saying by an Italian immigrant (whose name has been lost):

I came to America because I heard the streets were paved with gold. When I got here, I found out three things: first, the streets weren't paved with gold; second, they weren't paved at all; and third, I was supposed to pave them.

Chapter One: The Melting Pot

Immigrants came seeking economic opportunity, freedom from persecution, and adventure. Often, though, what they found was hard work, hard lives, and native-born Americans who were *not* very happy to see them.

There are several main arguments against immigration, and they have been made again and again throughout American history. One is that large numbers of immigrants will change the basic nature of the country. People argue that immigrants won't **assimilate**, but will instead make American culture more like their own. A related complaint is that immigrants are likely to vote for political

"The New Colossus"

Not like the brazen giant of Greek fame,
With conquering limbs astride from land to land;
Here at our sea-washed, sunset gates shall stand
A mighty woman with a torch, whose flame
Is the imprisoned lightning, and her name
Mother of Exiles. From her beacon-hand
Glows world-wide welcome; her mild eyes command
The air-bridged harbor that twin cities frame.

"Keep, ancient lands, your storied pomp!" cries she
With silent lips. "Give me your tired, your poor,
Your huddled masses yearning to breathe free,
The wretched refuse of your teeming shore.
Send these, the homeless, tempest-tost to me,
I lift my lamp beside the golden door!"

—Emma Lazarus (1883)

Immigrant Families

ANNUAL NUMBER OF U.S. LEGAL PERMANENT RESIDENTS

Year	New legal permanent residents	Year	New legal permanent residents
1830	23,322	1940	70,756
1840	84,066	1950	249,187
1850	369,980	1960	265,398
1860	153,640	1970	373,326
1870	387,203	1980	524,295
1880	457,257	1990	1,535,872
1890	455,302	2000	841,002
1900	448,572	2010	1,042,625
1910	1,041,570	2011	1,062,040
1920	430,001	2012	1,031,631
1930	241,700	2013	990,553

Note: Most recent data available as of publication date; these data represent people admitted for legal permanent residence during the year.
Source: Migration Policy Institute, "Legal Immigration to the United States, 1820–Present." http://www.migrationpolicy.org/programs/data-hub/charts/Annual-Number-of-US-Legal-Permanent-Residents.

candidates who will make the country "less free" or "less American." For example, the Order of the Star-Spangled Banner was founded in 1849 to protest immigration by Irish Catholics. Members of the order were nicknamed "Know-Nothings" because group membership was secret, and members would claim to "know nothing" about it. The Know-Nothings believed that Catholics could never be "real" Americans because of their religious beliefs.

Another argument against immigration is economic. The concern is that because immigrants are often willing to work for less money than other people, large numbers of immigrants will drive down wages for everyone else. For instance, Irish immigrants turned against Chinese immigrants in the late 18th century, in part because they thought the Chinese were competing with them for jobs building railroads. Discrimination against Chinese immigrants became

Chapter One: The Melting Pot   17

law in 1882, when the Chinese Exclusion Act prohibited new immigration from that country. (The law was not repealed until 1943.)

Some people who are against immigration also claim that immigrants are dangerous. They say immigrants are **illiterate**, violent, and more likely to commit crimes. In the 19th century, for example, some people blamed immigrants for increased alcoholism, and for the crime that went along with it. In California, meanwhile, Chinese immigrants were accused of being drug addicts.

A cartoon from *Frank Leslie's Illustrated Newspaper* in 1881. Titled "Know-Nothingism in Brooklyn," the image shows politicians turning away immigrants from a variety of countries, stating, "None but citizens of the United States can be licensed to engage in any employment in this city."

A poster in Colorado. Not everyone is accepting of recent immigrants who struggle with the language.

SOME THINGS NEVER CHANGE

Anti-immigration feelings tend to be **cyclical**. As mentioned above, when Irish Catholic immigrants arrived, some Protestant Americans objected. A generation later, the children of those Irish immigrants objected to newer Chinese immigrants. Historically, each ethnic group that has immigrated to America tends to want to "close the door behind them." *My group should come in*, they seem to argue, *but no more should follow.*

The arguments against immigration also tend to repeat themselves. Indeed, the arguments made in 1915 were extremely similar to the ones being made in 2015. In fact, it's likely you have heard these arguments on the news: immigrants change the culture, immigrants cause crime, immigrants take "our" jobs. All that really changes is the ethnic group being blamed.

Why does all of this matter? It matters because understanding the past is an important step toward understanding the present. Immigrant families today are affected by attitudes and beliefs that have been a part of American life for hundreds of years. The next chapters will look at what immigrant families look like today. You will probably notice that the challenges faced by immigrants in the 21st century are not so different from those faced by immigrants throughout history.

Text-Dependent Questions

1. What are some factors that might *push* people toward the United States?
2. What are some factors that *pull* them toward the United States?
3. Who were the Know-Nothings?

Research Project

Choose an ethnic group mentioned in this chapter and find out more about their immigration experience. When did it occur and what caused it? Was the immigration willing or unwilling? How were they greeted? Write a short history of your chosen group's immigration experience.

Immigrant Families

A naturalization ceremony, in which immigrants become American citizens.

Chapter Two

IMMIGRATION TODAY

In the 21st century, immigrants come to America from every corner of the world. And they don't just come to New York or California. Dearborn, Michigan, has the nation's largest population of Arab Americans. Saint Paul, Minnesota, has a large community of Hmong immigrants, many of whom fled Southeast Asia in the 1970s and 1980s. Along with its neighboring city, Minneapolis, it also has a large population of immigrants from Somalia, a country in eastern Africa. Harris County, Texas, where Houston is located, has more than 1 million immigrants, which is about a quarter of the total population.

Words to Understand

demographers: people who study population trends.

deported: sent back to one's country of origin.

fluctuate: to change often.

sociologists: people who study how large groups of people live.

UNDERSTANDING TERMS

As discussed in chapter one, almost all American families are immigrants if you look back far enough. But for practical purposes, the word *immigrant* is only applied to a person who left his or her country of origin and moved to a different one. **Demographers** also use the term *foreign-born* to describe that group of people. The opposite of *foreign-born* is *native-born*. If a family moves from another country to the United States and has children here, then the parents are foreign-born, while their children are native-born.

Immigrants are often called *first-generation*, meaning that they are the first generation of the family to settle and be established in the new country. Their

Three generations of an American family that has its roots in the Philippines.

Chapter Two: Immigration Today

Citizens and Noncitizens

In addition to the terms discussed here, a few others that are important. A *citizen* is someone who is a legal resident of a particular country. A citizen of a particular country might have been born in that country, or he or she might have gone through a legal process to become a citizen later in life (this is called *naturalization*). According to the U.S. Constitution, if someone is born in America (or in American-held territories), that person is a citizen. Citizens have certain rights and responsibilities simply because of that status.

A *noncitizen* is a guest in the country who may not have the same rights or responsibilities. Sometimes noncitizens are also called *aliens*. That term just means they come from a different country (not a different planet!). But saying that someone is a noncitizen or alien is *not* saying that he or she is in the country illegally. People from other countries come to the United States in a variety of ways. Noncitizens may only have permission to stay for a short period of time, or they may have permission to live here permanently. In fact, there are more than 13 million legal permanent residents in the United States. Some may go on to become full citizens, while others may not.

Discussions of immigration sometimes blend legal and illegal immigration together. It's important to remember that the two situations are not the same.

children are called *second-generation*. This is how the U.S. Census Bureau defines these terms, for example. However, not everyone agrees on that definition. Sometimes the term *first-generation* is used to describe only the immigrant's children—meaning the first ones to actually be born in the new country. So it can be confusing: first-generation can mean people who move to a new country, or it can mean the children of those people. For the purposes of this book, we will follow the U.S. Census Bureau, so that the word first-generation means foreign-born parents, and second-generation means their native-born children.

Case Study: Valentina and Brandi

Valentina was born in a rural part of Belarus called Pinsk, and she immigrated to Buffalo, New York, when she was a young girl. She was often frustrated by her parents' insistence that she live by the rules of "the old country." No make-up, no jeans, no earrings. Valentina was forever in dresses, forever plain, forever labeled an immigrant. She would never do that to her own daughter, she promised herself.

When she did have a daughter, Valentina gave her daughter a very American name, Brandi, and swore that Brandi would always speak English, never Russian. Brandi started kindergarten in jeans, a sweatshirt, and a pair of tiny pink sneakers. When Brandi was in middle school, she wanted a cell phone and other gadgets, just like all the other kids.

By this time, Valentina had gone back to school for a degree in psychology. One textbook described Southeast Asian families who immigrated to America but lost their connections to their old cultures. The age-old tradition of respect for elders was gone, and the children were separated from their rich cultural heritage. Valentina realized in shock that she had done the same thing, and she was encouraging more of the same in Brandi.

Slowly she introduced into her household the world she had known when she was young. Valentina began teaching Brandi how to speak a few words of Russian. Together, mother and daughter began to cook the ethnic dishes that Valentina remembered from her childhood. As a result, Brandi is still an American girl, but now she has a heritage uniquely her own.

Some **sociologists** use a third term, *Generation 1.5*, for young people who immigrated as kids. On the one hand, they grew up in the United States. They know the language and customs, and have many connections to this country. On the other hand, they also tend to retain knowledge of and contacts with their birth country. Members of Generation 1.5 combine aspects of both their birth country and their new one.

Importantly, because members of Generation 1.5 are foreign-born, they may not be citizens. This fact can make it very difficult for them to pursue their educations and find work. And if their parents brought them to America illegally, they are also vulnerable to arrest or deportation—even though they were not the ones who chose to immigrate.

STATISTICS ON IMMIGRANT FAMILIES

In 2013, there were more than 41.3 million immigrants in the United States. That was about 13 percent of the overall U.S. population at the time. Interestingly, that percentage is about the same as it was 100 years earlier. The percentage has **fluctuated** throughout history, however. It dropped below 10 percent during

According to a 2015 report, the United States now has about 41 million Spanish speakers, plus more than 11 million people who are bilingual in Spanish and English.

Illegal Immigration

In addition to the legal immigrants in the United States, there are other people who live in the country without the right permissions or paperwork. The Pew Research Organization estimates that there were about 11.3 million "unauthorized" immigrants living in the United States in 2014, or about 3.5 percent of the total population. The total number of undocumented immigrants has dropped from its record high of 12.2 million in 2007, and has been fairly stable since 2009.

Whether or not the issue of illegal immigration feels like a big problem might depend on where you live. Because, although the total number of undocumented immigrants has been stable recently, the number has gone up in some states, while dropping in others. Florida, Idaho, Maryland, Nebraska, New Jersey, Pennsylvania, and Virginia all saw increases in undocumented immigrants between 2009 and 2012. Meanwhile, 14 other states, including Alabama, Arizona, California, Illinois, Nevada, and New York, saw decreases during this period.

the 1930s and 1940s, for example. But speaking generally, the percentage of immigrants in the United States frequently hovers somewhere between 10 and 14 percent.

Immigrants from Mexico were the largest immigrant group in 2013—they made up 28 percent of the total immigrant population that year. Immigrants from India were the second most numerous (4.9 percent), followed by the Philippines (4.5 percent) and China (4.4 percent).

Approximately 17.4 million children under the age of 18 have at least one immigrant parent. That is about one quarter of all children in the United States. The vast majority of the kids are second-generation, meaning that they were born in the United States. Only about 12 percent (2.1 million) of immigrant kids are foreign-born themselves. The five states with the largest number of children living with immigrant parents are California (4.3 million); Texas (2.3 million); New York (1.5 million); Florida (1.2 million); and Illinois (784,000).

About 28 percent of adult immigrants have some type of college degree. That's only slightly lower than the native-born population—about 30 percent of native-born Americans have a college degree. Meanwhile, 30 percent of immigrants do not have a high school diploma. That number is noticeably higher than native-born Americans—only about 10 percent of American adults do not have a high school diploma.

REFUGEES

Chapter one talked about the history of immigration, and how some people were *pulled* to a new country by opportunity, while others were *pushed* there by trouble

The United States is far from the only country that accepts refugees. Here, Syrian and Iraqi refugees approach the border of Croatia, hoping to find safety in Western Europe.

Immigrant Families

Refugee Home Countries

Unfortunately, there are always refugees. But as wars and other crises begin and end, the source of these refugees changes over time. These are some of the countries and regions that have sent the largest number refugees to the United States:

- Former Soviet Union: 380,000 refugees
- Vietnam: 182,000 refugees
- Former Yugoslavia: 169,000 refugees
- Iraq: 106,000
- Myanmar (Burma): 104,000

Current refugee groups include Afghanistan, Rwanda, Syria, and Liberia.

in their home countries. The same thing is true today. Some immigrants come because they want to, while others come because they have to. The members of that second group are called refugees.

One particular group of refugees is worth noting: in the 2010s, there has been a huge jump in refugees fleeing gang violence in Mexico, El Salvador, Honduras, and Guatemala. Many of these refugees are children. Most are teenagers, but some are as young as five. They travel hundreds of miles in hopes of finding safety in the United States. In 2015 alone, 35,000 unaccompanied minors—meaning kids traveling without parents or other adult guardians—were caught at the border between the United States and Mexico. Children from Mexico are often sent back immediately, while kids from farther away are put in temporary shelters until they can be **deported**.

Refugees experience many of the same issues as other kinds of immigrants, such as learning the language and adjusting to a new culture. But refugee families frequently have other burdens as well. Most obviously, having to flee your home is a traumatic experience. Also, refugees often arrive with only the few possessions they can carry; this makes starting a new life even more difficult. Kids may also have lost loved ones or even be orphaned. Their educations have probably been interrupted, and it can be very challenging for them to focus on school.

Being a refugee can also be hard on kids socially. In one story related by the writer Christina Nuñez, a youth group in Utah invited some newly arrived refugee kids to join them on a camping trip. But halfway into the trip, the refugee kids became extremely upset. It turned out that hiking through the desert brought back terrible memories of having to flee their homes.

Text-Dependent Questions

1. What are the two different meanings of "first-generation immigrant"?
2. Name two states where illegal immigration has increased, and two where it has decreased.
3. What makes refugees different from immigrants?

Research Project

Write a report about immigrant groups in your neighborhood, town, or state. What are the main countries they come from? What spurred them to immigrate?

30 Immigrant Families

Immigrants crowded into an English-language class at the Ford Motor Company, circa 1920s.

Chapter Three
THE SALAD BOWL

In 1914, the Ford Motor Company was one of America's largest employers. More than three-quarters of the employees were foreign-born. Many were recent immigrants who did not speak English or have much understanding of American culture. So Henry Ford created the Ford English School, which provided not only language lessons, but also instruction in "American values."

The company also had a Sociological Department, which set rules that employees had to follow—not just on the job, but at home, too. For example, inspectors would visit the employees in their company-owned houses and make sure they were clean. As Elana Firsht wrote in the *Michigan Journal of History*, Ford hoped to "turn out Americans in the same way he mass-produced cars."

Ford's programs might seem strange today, but they reflected ideas that were widely held at that time. People believed there was really only one way to be "an American," and they thought everyone should try to live up to that

> ### Words to Understand
>
>
> **acculturation:** the process of adapting to a new culture.
>
> **discrimination:** being treated less well than everyone else, because of the group you belong to.
>
> **multiculturalism:** the belief that different cultures should be celebrated.

standard. People also believed in total assimilation for immigrants. That is, they believed that when immigrants arrived in the country, they should forget their old customs and adopt new "American" ones. American customs were considered to be more valuable than the customs of immigrants' home countries.

ADAPTING AND ADJUSTING

We view things a bit differently today. People are more likely to talk about **acculturation** than about assimilation. The two words are very similar, but acculturation implies that immigrants can adapt to their new home while *also* retaining aspects of their old culture. It's been said that America should not be a "melting pot," in which everyone is the same, but a "salad bowl," in which cultures are together but distinct, the way ingredients in a salad are.

Immigrants are not the only ones who benefit from acculturation. The culture as a whole can become richer and more interesting when people are allowed to be unique. Food is a great example of this. Depending on where you live, you

The main street of Chinatown in San Francisco.

Chapter Three: The Salad Bowl

Chinese Food

What Americans call Chinese food is pretty different from what people in China actually eat.

Culture does not only travel in one direction. Immigrants affect the culture of their new country, and the new country also affects the immigrants. Immigrant parents pass their cultural traditions on to their children, in the hopes that although their kids are Americans, they will also remember where their family came from. One very common way for culture to be transferred is through food. But as immigrants bring their recipes to their new country, those recipes evolve over time.

For example, what you know as Chinese food is actually very different from what people eat in China. This "American" Chinese food was developed to appeal to the American fondness for sugar and salt. It also uses foods that aren't native to China, like broccoli. Some dishes in Chinese restaurants were invented in America, such as chop suey. Others, like sweet-and-sour sauce, did originate in China, but have now been changed so much that they are hardly the same thing any more.

Interestingly, American sweet-and-sour sauce is now popular in China. In fact, the country has an American-style Chinese food restaurant in Shanghai. There, the cuisine is called "American food," and Chinese chefs have to be specially trained to prepare these strange dishes. As the restaurant owner Fung Lam told one reporter, "In China they like the bones, but we had the staff spend hours deboning the chicken. They were saying, 'Why are we doing this?' We also got them to fill wontons with cheese. [The cooks] were thinking, *What is going on?*"

may have a variety of different restaurants close by. Chinese, Mexican, Italian, Japanese, Thai, and Indian are just some of the ethnic foods that Americans love—and they were all brought by immigrants.

Like the United States, Canada also has a large immigrant population. People immigrate to Canada from all over the world; the most common source countries are the Philippines, India, China, and Iran. But Canada has long been more devoted to the "salad bowl" idea, rather than the melting pot. A 1938 book, *Canadian Mosaic*, by the Scottish Canadian writer Joel Murray Gibbon, was very critical of American assimilation, and it influenced generations of Canadians. In the 1970s, **multiculturalism** became official government policy in Canada. There is even a law, the Canadian Multiculturalism Act (1988), that protects the rights of cultural minorities.

CONCERNS ABOUT MULTICULTURALISM

Most people do not expect immigrants to completely abandon their traditions the way they did in Henry Ford's day. But even so, multiculturalism is controversial to some extent.

First, not assimilating can actually be bad for immigrant families financially. For example, sociologists have noted that Mexican immigrants often have low levels of "economic acculturation." This term refers to how much the immigrant is able to participate in and benefit from the larger economy. It affects things like what jobs people can get, how much they earn, and whether they can start their own businesses. A low level of economic acculturation can make it harder for people to improve their lives, because they are shut out of the better-paying jobs and opportunities.

Some people also worry that multiculturalism creates a sense of separateness—that it focuses too much on how people are different, rather than how they are alike. The fear is that we will lose the culture that connects us, and that being "American" or "Canadian" will no longer mean anything. This can be especially tough on immigrant children who want to be part of their new culture. Often, they feel their parents and grandparents pulling them back to the culture and values of their home country.

Chapter Three: The Salad Bowl

The concern about assimilation became especially strong in 2015, due to terrorist attacks in France and the United States. If immigrants do not assimilate, the argument goes, they will not come to love their new country. This may make them more easily convinced to commit acts of violence.

These concerns are understandable, and they are shared by many anti-terrorism experts. But it's worth noting that these arguments are very similar to the fears people have had in the past. Back in the 19th century, people feared that Irish immigrants were not assimilating well. In the 20th century, Italian, German, and Japanese immigrants all faced **discrimination** during periods of war between the United States and their home countries.

In Canada, signs are frequently posted in two languages because the country has so many French speakers.

Text-Dependent Questions

1. What's the difference between assimilation and acculturation?
2. What is multiculturalism?
3. What are some fears people have about multiculturalism?

Research Project

Write an essay that explains the difference between the "melting pot" and the "salad bowl" concepts. Choose which model you think is better for immigrant families in the United States, and defend your opinion in your essay.

36 Immigrant Families

The younger kids are, the easier it is for them to pick up a new language.

Chapter Four

CHALLENGES FOR IMMIGRANT FAMILIES

Every family is different, so it's impossible to say that *all* immigrant families experience the same problems. Where immigrants come from has a big impact on how easily they assimilate. So does where they live once they immigrate. People who move to neighborhoods that already have a lot of immigrants may find the transition easier. But there are some general problem areas that most immigrant families will have to deal with.

LEARNING THE LANGUAGE

When immigrants arrive in their new country, one of the first things they encounter is a new language. According to the Migration Policy Institute, 79 percent of the U.S.

Words to Understand

hijab: a head covering worn by many Muslim girls and women.

linguists: people who study languages.

proficient: skilled at something.

population speaks only English at home, and 21 percent of the population speaks another language. Spanish is the most common, followed by Chinese and then Vietnamese. Of the total number of immigrants, about half are considered limited English **proficient** (LEP), which means they may speak some English, but they do not speak it "very well."

How difficult it is for immigrants to learn a new language depends on a number of factors. One major factor is age. Kids almost always have an easier time learning a new language than adults do. Kids often have to help their parents or grandparents in tasks that require the use of the new language. Another factor has to do with what their native language is. **Linguists** have found that certain languages are easier for people to learn because the sounds are similar. People who speak Spanish or German might have an easier time learning English than people who speak Vietnamese or Thai. That's simply because the first two languages are similar in some ways with English, while the second two are not. Vietnamese and Thai don't even use the alphabet that English does.

It's a given that some level of English knowledge is necessary in order to get by in the United States. In a report from the Robert Wood Johnson Foundation, immigrants share stories of how difficult it can be to simply buy food in a store, fill out a form, or understand a bus schedule when they don't know the language. One Chinese immigrant explained his frustration about the time he was in a car accident but was unable to tell a police officer what happened. Meanwhile, some U.S. communities have declared themselves to be "English Only." These communities refuse to translate signs, government forms, or documents.

GETTING AN EDUCATION

Most immigrant families would probably agree that their kids' education is very precious. In fact, the chance to give their kids a better life is a key reason why many families immigrate in the first place. But that doesn't mean that getting that education is always easy.

Chapter Four: Challenges for Immigrant Families

One challenge, as noted above, is language. Kids often pick up the language of their new country faster than their parents. This is great, but it can make it almost impossible for parents to help kids with their homework. Parents may also have trouble talking to teachers, or they may be too intimidated to do so.

Sometimes parents are confused by or downright unhappy with the way American schools are run. They may be used to different styles of teaching or stricter discipline, for example. They may be confused or worried by the pop culture that their kids are exposed to at school.

As for the immigrant kids themselves, their school experiences can vary a great deal, depending on which generation they are. First-generation kids, who are born in one country and then dropped into a new one, often struggle to

Immigrant parents may feel intimidated about speaking to their child's teacher.

Newcomer Pitfalls

The website Colorín Colorado (http://www.colorincolorado.org) offers lots of information to help educators who interact with large numbers of recent arrivals to the United States. In a post called "Lessons Learned from Immigrant Families" (http://www.colorincolorado.org/article/lessons-learned-immigrant-families), Maryland educator Young-Chan Han offers the following advice to teachers:

- Don't assume new families are familiar with American school traditions. Things that may seem obvious to you might not be obvious to someone else. Not all countries have school buses, for example. An immigrant family may not know what school buses are or how to find one. They may not understand how to fill out a particular form, or the meaning of a two-hour delay in a school opening during bad weather.
- Remember that food is cultural. If you are offering snacks, consider if they are appropriate. In one example, pizza was given to recent immigrants from Burma. But like many Asians, Burmese people do not normally eat dairy, and they were surprised and confused by this new food.
- Consider if homework assignments are understandable to immigrant parents. Be patient if it takes the parents time to understand how they can help their kids succeed in school.

keep up academically. On the other hand, sociologists find that second-generation kids—those who are native-born to foreign-born parents—tend to be pretty much like any other American kid. However, they may still experience bullying because of cultural differences. Other kids might pick on their clothes, for example, or the "strange" food they bring from home.

Some ethnicities are especially targeted. In the Robert Wood Johnson Foundation report, one Arab immigrant student noted, "I wear the **hijab** in school and some people try and tell me to take it off. . . . They keep on telling me

Chapter Four: Challenges for Immigrant Families

to take it off, and then I say I can't take it off . . . so then they say, 'so is your father [a terrorist]?'"

Even kids who don't have to deal with the "terrorist" label still face discrimination in small ways. Sometimes it comes from people who mean well but just don't know any better. For example, nearly every child of immigrants has at some point had to deal with the question, "Where are you from?" That's a pretty frustrating question for a second-generation immigrant who was born in the United States! The answer, of course, is: "I'm from America, just like you are!"

Unfortunately, kids who dress differently from what's considered "normal" may face teasing or discrimination at school.

FAMILY DYNAMICS

The TV show *Master of None*, which debuted in 2015, features two best friends: one is the son of Indian immigrants, and the other is the son of Chinese immigrants. Part of the show revolves around the tensions between first-generation immigrants, who've struggled throughout their lives, and their children, who live in comfort. In one episode, the younger characters try to come to terms with how different their parents' lives have been. "What an insane journey," one says. "My dad used to bathe in a river; now he has a car that talks to him."

This is a situation that most immigrant families will recognize. Immigrants work hard to provide better lives for their children. But they are sometimes surprised at how different—how American—their kids turn out to be. As kids begin to blend in with their new culture, they sometimes start to seem like strangers to their parents—and their parents often don't like it!

Immigrant parents want their kids to succeed in America, but most hope they will not forget their cultural background, either.

Chapter Four: Challenges for Immigrant Families

It can be hard for kids and parents to understand each other sometimes. On the one hand, parents want and expect their kids to succeed in their new country. Indeed, gaining opportunities for their kids is a big reason why many people immigrate in the first place. But sometimes that success comes at a cost. Kids might not value the same things as their parents, or they may not see the world in quite the same way. So, yes, parents want their kids to succeed in America. But at the same time, they sometimes worry about their kids becoming "too American."

Also, when a child knows more about the new language or culture, it creates an imbalance in power between the grown-up and the kid. In other words, parents may need to rely on their kids to do basic things like buying groceries or answering the phone. That's an extremely uncomfortable situation for most adults, who expect to be the ones in charge.

An important thing to remember if you are struggling with these issues is that you are not alone. Remember the number given earlier in this book: there are more than 41 million immigrants in the United States, or about 13 percent of the population. So lots of people are going through the same cultural adjustments. The fact is, America would not be the country it is without its immigrants—and that includes you and your family!

Text-Dependent Questions

1. What does LEP mean?
2. What are some challenges that kids face at school?
3. What are some challenges for immigrant parents and their kids?

Research Project

Find out what services your school and community offer to newcomers. Create a poster or flyer that explains how immigrants can access these services.

FURTHER READING

Books

Gonzalez, Ana Lucia. "Hispanics in the US: Generation 1.5." BBC News, June 10, 2010. http://www.bbc.com/news/10209099.

Kenney, Karen. *Illegal Immigration*. Essential Viewpoints. Edina, MN: ABDO, 2007.

Landau, Elaine. *Ellis Island*. New York: Children's Press, 2008.

Sandler, Martin W. *Immigrants*. A Library of Congress Book. New York: HarperCollins, 1995.

Online

Migration Policy Institute. "Children in U.S. Immigrant Families." http://www.migrationpolicy.org/programs/data-hub/charts/children-immigrant-families.

U.S. Committee for Refugees and Immigrants. "Refugees." http://refugees.org/explore-the-issues/our-work-with-refugees.

Get Help Now

National Immigrant Justice Center

"Resources for Immigrant Children and Young Adults." This web page provides manuals in many languages about the legal rights of child immigrants.
https://www.immigrantjustice.org/resources-immigrant-children-and-young-adults

SERIES GLOSSARY

agencies: departments of a government with responsibilities for specific programs.

anxiety: a feeling of worry or nervousness.

biological parents: the woman and man who create a child; they may or not raise it.

caregiving: helping someone with their daily activities.

cognitive: having to do with thinking or understanding.

consensus: agreement among a particular group of people.

custody: legal guardianship of a child.

demographers: people who study information about people and communities.

depression: severe sadness or unhappiness that does not go away easily.

discrimination: singling out a group for unfair treatment.

disparity: a noticeable difference between two things.

diverse: having variety; for example, "ethnically diverse" means a group of people of many different ethnicities.

ethnicity: a group that has a shared cultural heritage.

extended family: the kind of family that includes members beyond just parents and children, such as aunts, uncles, cousins, and so on.

foster care: raising a child (usually temporarily) that is not adopted or biologically yours.

heir: someone who receives another person's wealth and social position after the other person dies.

homogenous: a group of things that are the same.

ideology: a set of ideas and ways of seeing the world.

incarceration: being confined in prison or jail.

inclusive: accepting of everyone.

informally: not official or legal.

institution: an established organization, custom, or tradition.

kinship: family relations.

neglect: not caring for something correctly.

patriarchal: a system that is run by men and fathers.

prejudice: beliefs about a person or group based only on simplified and often mistaken ideas.

prevalence: how common a particular trait is in a group of people.

psychological: having to do with the mind.

quantify: to count or measure objectively.

restrictions: limits on what someone can do.

reunification: putting something back together.

secular: nonreligious.

security: being free from danger.

social worker: a person whose job is to help families or children deal with particular problems.

socioeconomic: relating to both social factors (such as race and ethnicity) as well as financial factors (such as class).

sociologists: people who study human society and how it operates.

spectrum: range.

stability: the sense that things will stay the same.

stereotype: a simplified idea about a type of person that is not connected to actual individuals.

stigma: a judgment that something is bad or shameful.

stressor: a situation or event that causes upset (stress).

traumatic: something that's very disturbing and causes long-term damage to a person.

variable: something that can change.

INDEX

Page numbers in *italics* refer to photographs or tables.

acculturation   31, 32–34

advice for teachers   40

assimilation   15, *30,* 31–32

California Gold Rush   13

Canada, immigration and   34, *35*

Canadian Multiculturalism Act (1988)   34

Chinese Exclusion Act (1882)   17

Chinese immigration   13, 16–*17*, 33

citizen vs noncitizen   23

de Argüelles, Jr., Martín   11

deportation   21, 25, 28

discrimination   16–18, 39–41

English language   37–39

first generation, definition of   22–23

food, immigration and   32–34

Ford, Henry   31

Generation 1.5   24–25

hijab   40, *41*

home countries   26, 28

illegal immigration   23, 26

immigrants, education and   38–40
   numbers of   12, 16, 21, 25–27, 43
   controversy over   14–19
   history of   12–14, 35
   parents and kids   42–43

Know-Nothings   16, *17*

Lazarus, Emma   12, 15

legal permanent residents   16, 23

multiculturalism   32–35

refugees   27–29
   children   28–29

second generation, definition of   22–23

St. Augustine, Florida   11, 12

Statue of Liberty   *10,* 12

ABOUT THE AUTHOR

H. W. Poole is a writer and editor of books for young people, including the 13-volume set, *Mental Illnesses and Disorders: Awareness and Understanding* (Mason Crest). She created the *Horrors of History* series (Charlesbridge) and the *Ecosystems* series (Facts On File). She has also been responsible for many critically acclaimed reference books, including *Political Handbook of the World* (CQ Press) and the *Encyclopedia of Terrorism* (SAGE). She was coauthor and editor of *The History of the Internet* (ABC-CLIO), which won the 2000 American Library Association RUSA award.

PHOTO CREDITS

Photos are for illustrative purposes only; individuals depicted are models.
Cover: Dollar Photo Club/Monkey Business
iStock.com: 6 MordorIff; 9 Den Kuvaiev; 10 OlegAlbinsky; 20 P_Wei; 22 azndc; 25 LifesizeImages; 27 MilosMalinic; 32 zodebala; 33 zimmytws; 35 OliverChilds; 36 monkeybusinessimages; 39 Steve Debenport; 41 valeriebarry; 42 IanVorster
Library of Congress: 13; 14; 17; 30
Wikimedia Commons: 18 CGP Grey